I Have a Question about Death

of related interest

Talking About Death and Bereavement in School
How to Help Children Aged 4 to 11 to Feel
Supported and Understood
Ann Chadwick
ISBN 978 1 84905 246 7
eISBN 978 0 85700 527 4

**Helping Children with Autism Spectrum
Conditions through Everyday Transitions**
Small Changes – Big Challenges
John Smith, Jane Donlan and Bob Smith
ISBN 978 1 84905 275 7
eISBN 978 0 85700 572 4

The Disappointment Dragon
Learning to cope with disappointment (for all children and
dragon tamers, including those with Asperger Syndrome)
K.I. Al-Ghani
Illustrated by Haitham Al-Ghani
ISBN 978 1 84905 432 4
eISBN 978 0 85700 780 3

Great Answers to Difficult Questions about Death
What Children Need to Know
Linda Goldman
ISBN 978 1 84905 805 6
eISBN 978 1 84642 957 6

I Have a Question about Death

A Book for Children with Autism Spectrum Disorder or Other Special Needs

Arlen Grad Gaines and Meredith Englander Polsky

Jessica Kingsley Publishers
London and Philadelphia

First published in 2017
by Jessica Kingsley Publishers
73 Collier Street
London N1 9BE, UK
and
400 Market Street, Suite 400
Philadelphia, PA 19106, USA

www.jkp.com

Library of Congress Cataloging in Publication Data
.A CIP catalog record for this book is available from the Library of Congress

British Library Cataloguing in Publication Data
A CIP catalogue record for this book is available from the British Library

ISBN 978 1 78592 750 8
eISBN 978 1 78450 545 5

Printed and bound in China

For Brian, Jaden, and Casey,
and Adam, Hayden, Lucy, and Emma

In memory of Edith Krohn and
Shulamith Kustanowitz

Acknowledgments

With tremendous gratitude to Suzanne Adelman, Liane Carter, Dr. Caren Glassman, Rae Grad, Benay Josselson, Laura Meyn, Manny Schiffres, and Stephanie Slater for their feedback and encouragement. Thank you to our caring and compassionate colleagues at JSSA Hospice and Matan.

Our families have supported us from the beginning, and we truly could not have written this book without them. A special thank you to Jaden Gaines for his superb editorial assistance.

Thank you to Jessica Kingsley, Elen Griffiths, and the staff at Jessica Kingsley Publishers for their kind guidance and collaboration.

Preface

As clinicians working in the fields of hospice social work and special education, we meet countless families of children with Autism Spectrum Disorder or other special needs as they grapple with how to process the death of a loved one. We wrote *I Have a Question about Death* to provide children, families, and professionals with a book that addresses death and grief in concrete and accessible ways, while acknowledging that some questions do not have satisfying answers.

We hope this book serves as a resource for all children, including concrete thinkers, children who struggle with anxiety, and siblings of children with special needs. We offer it as a resource for therapists, clinicians, educators, and pediatricians, as they address the needs of the families they serve.

I Have a Question about Death consists of three components:

1. The complete story
Created with straightforward text and clear illustrations for children who process information best through words and pictures.

2. Short picture story
Designed for children who learn best through visual cues, and those who may want to re-read the story and think about it independently.

3. Suggestions for parents and caregivers
Written for the adults in a child's life, helping them continue the conversation about death and dying.

Hi! I'm a kid who likes a lot of things. I like to do puzzles, read books, and play on the computer.

I'm also a kid who likes to know what to expect each day. Most of the time, that works out fine.

Most days are regular days. They go like this:

I wake up. I have breakfast. I brush my teeth and my hair. I get dressed for school and I walk to the bus.

I see my teachers and friends and work hard. In the afternoon, I come home, do my homework, and play at my house. I take a shower (most nights!), eat dinner, and go to sleep.

Once in a while, though, something different happens and the day doesn't go the way I expect.

Today was one of those days. I learned something new. I learned that someone I love has died.

I really wasn't expecting that.

Now I have *a lot* of questions. I'm a kid who likes when there are answers to my questions. Today, I'm asking my questions and some of them have answers. But some of them don't.

"What does it mean when a person dies?"
That is my first question. It has an answer.

When someone dies, it means their body stops working. Their heart stops beating. Their lungs stop breathing. When someone dies, they are not sleeping. They are not eating. They are not hearing. When someone dies, they never stop being dead.

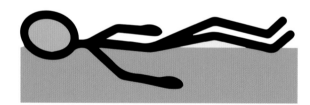

Next I want to know, *"Why do people die?"*

I learn that people die for lots of different reasons. Most of the time when people die, they are old and have lived a long life. But not always. Sometimes people who are not old get very sick or hurt.

Doctors can usually help people get better, but not always. Nobody can really answer why people die if they are young and haven't lived a long life.

It's hard not to know the answer to this question. I like it better when questions have answers.

"Does it hurt to die?" I ask.

Doctors try really hard to make sure that people who are dying are not in pain. They give them special medicine. Usually when doctors give people medicine, it helps them get better. When people are dying, medicine can't make them better, but it can help to take away any pain.

"What happens to people when they die?"
I want to know.

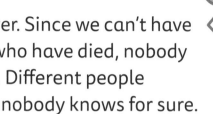

There isn't a very good answer. Since we can't have conversations with people who have died, nobody really knows what happens. Different people believe different things, but nobody knows for sure.

Maybe my next question will have a better answer.

"But what about the person's body?"
I'm so curious.

Different families have different traditions. Sometimes the person's body goes into a box called a coffin. The coffin is placed in the ground. That's called a grave. Sometimes the person's body is cremated, which means it is turned into ash. It doesn't hurt to be buried or cremated because the person is not alive anymore.

Many people have a ceremony to remember the person who died. It's called a funeral or a memorial service.

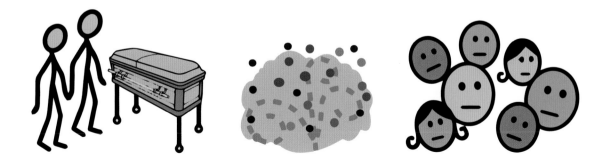

"When someone dies, what does it feel like for the people who are still alive?"

When someone dies, people feel very sad. They are sad because they miss the person who died. They wish they could see them again.

I see some people crying, so I know they are sad. I feel like crying, too. It's okay to cry when I feel sad.

I also see some people laughing and that is confusing! I learn that they are remembering a nice or funny story about the person who died. I feel like laughing, too. It's okay to laugh even after someone I love has died. When I laugh, I feel less sad.

I find out that sometimes there are a lot of people around after someone has died. It can feel noisy, and people might try to hug me a lot. I don't have to ask about any of that. I see it for myself!

Now I know it's okay for me to take a break, or go to a quiet space and come back when I feel ready.

"What can I do when someone I love has died?"

When someone has died, I can think about their life and what we liked to do together. I can talk about that person, how nice they were, and why I loved being with them. Sometimes looking at pictures and thinking about them might make me feel sad, sometimes happy, and sometimes both.

"When someone I love has died, will I ever see them again?"

When someone I love has died, I will not see them any more. I will always love them, though. I might think about them when I do something that they liked to do. That's a good way to remember someone who has died.

I know there are many people who love me. It's okay if I want to talk about the person who died, and it's also okay if I don't.

Even after someone dies, I will have regular days
again. I will still wake up, eat my breakfast, and
go to school. Sometimes I might think about the
person who died. I might think of more questions to
ask. Now I know that a lot of my questions will have
answers, but some of them won't.

Most days are regular days. Most days I know just what to expect. Today was not a regular day, but I learned a lot. Mostly I learned that asking questions really helps!

Short Picture Story:
I Have a Question about Death

On the pages that follow, you will see the same pictures used in the story along with shorter, more direct text. This is a tool for children who learn best through visual cues, and for children who might want to re-read and think about the story independently.

Hi!

I like puzzles.

I like to read.

I like computers.

 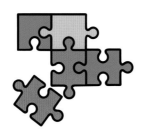  

Most days are the same.

I go to school.

I see my friends.

I come home at the end of the day.

Today is different. Someone I love died.

I have a lot of questions.

What does it mean when someone dies?

Their body stopped working.

Why did they die?

Usually they're old, but not always.

Nobody really knows why people die if they're not old.

Does it hurt to die?

No. Doctors try hard to make sure it doesn't hurt.

What happens to the person who dies?

People believe different things.

What about the person's body?

Sometimes there is a coffin and sometimes there are ashes.

Often there is a funeral or memorial service.

What about the people who are still alive?

People feel sad.

Why are people laughing?

They are remembering a funny story.

It can feel noisy.

People may want to hug me.

I can take a break.

What can I do when someone dies?

I can think about them.

I can talk about them.

Will I see the person again?

No. But I can remember things we liked to do together.

Lots of people love me.

I will have regular days again.

Asking questions really helps!

Suggestions for Parents and Caregivers

As with all children, those with Autism Spectrum Disorder or other special needs will be affected in some way by the death of a loved one. Although some parents and caregivers may be inclined to shield children from information and conversations about the death, it can be helpful to include them in ways that take into account their specific developmental, social, and emotional learning needs. Here are some suggestions for parents and caregivers to help a child with special needs understand and process the death of a loved one.

Use clear language

Many children with special needs process information in a concrete manner. Try to use the actual words, such as "died," rather than "passed away" or "gone." Though these softer words can feel to adults like they are cushioning the topic, they may make it less comprehensible to a child for whom euphemisms are difficult.

Prepare for next steps

If the child is attending the funeral or memorial service, help plan for that in advance. Think about strategies that have worked in other aspects of the child's life, and apply those to this experience as well (a picture schedule or check-list of the day's activities, for example). Arrange for a trusted adult to be available to give the child a break, if needed, during this time.

Prepare for a range of emotions

Some children with special needs may have difficulty reading the emotions of others. Let them know that people may be crying because they are sad. Explain that sometimes they may be laughing when sharing a funny story about the person who died. Remind them that people may want to hug and kiss them. Prepare them for the range of feelings they may experience.

Provide structure and routine

As far as possible, maintain familiar routines. They contribute to a sense of safety and normality and can be comforting to the child.

Prepare for the possibility of regression

Know ahead of time that all children, including those with special needs, may regress or turn to self-soothing behaviors after a loved one has died. Help provide the types of support, such as a preferred activity, quiet time, or sensory-friendly opportunities, that have proven successful in other areas of the child's life.

Remember the loved one

Find accessible and meaningful ways to remember the person who died. For instance, if the child is drawn to wheels, remind him or her of a shared experience, such as when they played cars together.

Provide guidance to the child in remembering their relationship with the person who died. Ideas include sharing a photo of the child and the loved one, or working together to create a memory book or box.

Support the child

Utilize the support of people who are already involved in the child's life. Be sure to inform counselors, teachers, and therapists of the death so they can partner with you in supporting the child.

Arlen Grad Gaines is a licensed clinical social worker based in Maryland, USA. With a decade's experience in hospice social work, she has developed a specialization in supporting families who have children with special needs around the subject of death and dying.

Meredith Englander Polsky has been working in social work and special education for more than 15 years and lives in Maryland, USA. She founded Matan, Inc. (www.matankids.org) in 2000, which has helped improve Jewish education around special needs for tens of thousands of families.